ANOINT ME, LORD

Brenda B. Matthews

Bea-Mor Publishing

Copyright © 2013 Brenda B. Matthews

All Rights Reserved

No part of this book may be reproduced, or stored in a retrieval system, or transmitted in any form or by any means, electronic, mechanical, photocopying, recording, or otherwise, without express written permission of the publisher.

Email: brendabmatthews@att.net

ISBN-13: 9780989136822
ISBN-10: 0989236825

Printed in the United States of America

References:
The Pastor's Wife Does Cry, Lady Bea Morgan
Walking in Righteousness, Brenda B. Matthews
HumblingThyself, Brenda B. Matthews
If I Were a Man and Had a Wife, Brenda B. Matthews
Ladyb Bea Morgan, The Extension, Lady Bea Morgan

Cover Design by LaRahn Michael

Editor: Pastor Cassandra McDonald

CONTENTS

Title Page	1
Copyright	2
Preface	5
Anoint vs. Anointing	9
STRONGHOLDS	14
Anoint Me, Prayer!	15
Anoint My Head, Lord	16
Anoint My Mind, Lord	18
Anoint My Eyes, Lord	22
Anoint My Ears, Lord	26
Anoint My Mouth, Lips, and Tongue, Lord	30
Anoint My Hands, Lord	35
Anoint My Feet, Lord	39
Anoint Me, Lord	42
After We Pray	45

PREFACE

There is power in prayer. We have to be creative, consistent, and strategic with prayers. Usually, we have others to pray with us or for us, laying hands upon us; where two or three gather together in Jesus' name, there He is in the midst, Matthew 18:20.

Anoint Me Lord was written for you to pour blessed oil into your hands, then place them on parts of your body as the facilitator directs you in prayer, even if you are the facilitator.

Use these prayers during public prayer services, shut-ins, conferences, retreats, convocations, bible classes, councils, or during personal private prayer sessions.

Couple the prayers with fasting and witness manifestations of the Lord!

Lord, remind us that to witness Your works and empowerment, faith must be activated.

Lord remind us that we all have a measure of faith. Some have no faith, some have little faith, some have mountain moving faith, some have mustard seed faith, some have wavering faith, some have dead faith, some have great faith, and some have the gift of faith.

Nevertheless, use your measure!

Expect miracles!

Be Blessed!

Brenda B. Matthews

ANOINT ME, LORD
Brenda B. Matthews

ANOINT VS. ANOINTING

God's power is the anointing.

The anointing comes for a purpose; it comes to do work. When the power of God, the anointing, is present, people are healed of sickness, disease, infirmities, and delivered from personal strongholds.

It is the power of God, the anointing, needed to cast out demons, loosen shackles, bind and loosen spirits, break yokes of bondage, awaken churches, strengthen spirits, and frighten enemies. The work of the anointing is visible evidence of the presence of the Lord.

It is the power of God, the anointing, needed in prayer, for God to move mightily.

It is the power of God, the anointing, needed to preach the word of God.

It is the power of God, the anointing, needed to teach the word of God.

It is the power of God, the anointing, needed to receive the preached word of God.

It is the power of God, the anointing, needed to convict

us and correct us of wrongdoing (sins).

It is the power of God, the anointing, needed to change our heart and mind to work in righteousness.

It is the power of God, the anointing, needed to pray for others, whether interceding, privately, or publicly.

It is the power of God, the anointing, needed for us to move when God says move.

It is the power of God, the anointing, needed to speak when God says to speak.

It is the power of God, the anointing, needed to sing songs of deliverance.

It is the power of God, the anointing, needed to encourage others.

It is the power of God, the anointing, needed to prophesy.

It is the power of God, the anointing, needed to allow us to move by His voice, to comfort others, instruct others, or to follow His leading.

It is the power of God, the anointing, needed to bring forth fruit (witness).

It is the power of God, the anointing, needed to possess the fullness of joy.

As you learn more of God, He will show you His mysteries. He will show you other means of identifying His presence and His power.

Below defines *anoint* and the *anointing*, explaining the difference in being anointed by man versus being anointed by Jesus Christ.

ANOINT – To rub or sprinkle oil on; to consecrate or make sacred with oil

ANOINT – Power; The power from God

ANOINTING – The power of God

Whom would you desire to anoint you, man or Jesus?

Do "Man" and "Jesus" possess the same power?

Would your request be "Anoint me John" or "Anoint me Jesus?"

Does it matter who anoints you as long as you are anointed?

If I say, "Lord, anoint me," will the Lord place blessed oil upon me?

If I say, "John, anoint me," will John infuse power upon me?

Is the power in the blessed oil?

Or

Is the power in Jesus?

Is your faith in that "special touch" from John as he administers blessed oil upon you?

Or

Is your faith in that "touch" from God?

When you personally say, "I'm anointed," which anoint are you referring to?

Do you mean you have blessed oil on you or do you mean Jesus is upon you?

When blessed oil is administered, what is symbolized or what is happening? It symbolizes the power from God. There is a distinct difference between a "Special Touch" and the "Touch".

When man places blessed oil upon us, the faith we have in Jesus is activated.

We believe and we are in agreement with "man" as to

the reason "man" is placing blessed oil upon us. The "power" which is the "anointing" is Jesus, not the man himself. However, the **power** or the **anointing** can be present upon the man or inside the man administering the blessed oil, but the power "alone" is all Jesus Christ.

Remember, the anointing comes to do a work that no man can do with his hands. It does a work that only Jesus Himself can!

STRONGHOLDS

Strongholds are mind binders; keeping untruths locked in the mind, though the truth is presented. At the same time, they block truths from entering the mind. Strongholds keeps us from receiving the truth. They separate us from God. Sometimes we get assistance in blocking us from the truth through the influence of unsaved friends, relatives, saints, television, books, newspapers, etc. If we continue to believe a lie, Satan has a stronghold on us. Analogy: If several trusting people continuously tell you the same thing and prove to you that what you believe is not true, but you insist on believing what you believe, look further into it; you may have a stronghold. Many times, our enemies are not our enemies. We have spent countless years believing certain people dislike us based upon hearsay or based upon erroneous thinking. Sometimes we walk in on the end of a conversation, assuming we were the topic and discussed negatively. This forms bitterness towards the entire group. Once the matter is brought to the forefront, truth is revealed. When the truth is revealed, but the untruth is still believed, we are now facing a stronghold. Sometimes we can view people a certain way, concoct in our mind numerous unpleasant images, and then create a strong dislike for the person for years. Every time the person is seen or thought of, unease is present. Again, when untruth is believed, rather than the truth, a stronghold is at hand. One thing about a stronghold is that it can be pulled down through fervent and effectual prayer, in the name of Jesus.

We have to make sure God, who is all truth, is our stronghold. The LORD is good, a stronghold in the day of trouble; and he knoweth them that trust in him, Nahum 1:7.

ANOINT ME, PRAYER!

Dear Lord, as I place blessed oil upon my body, empower me so I may do a greater work for You; so I may experience a greater work of You through me. With Your anointing upon me and penetrating through me, I will be empowered to speak with more authority, walk with more boldness, and intercede in prayer suddenly. Lord, Your presence resting upon me will pull down strongholds, loosen shackles, cast out demons, heal the sick and the infirmed, save souls, raise the dead, instill truth, lift up bowed down heads, tremble demons, convict and not condemn, feed the spiritually hungry and thirsty souls all in the Name of Jesus Christ of Nazareth and all for Your Glory!

ANOINT MY HEAD, LORD

Jesus, as I place oil upon myself:

Anoint my head, Lord so the power will trickle down my entire body lingering in the atmosphere as I walk, blessing everyone nearby.

Anoint my head, Lord so it is lifted above my enemies who are around me so when their fiery darts are thrown, they will witness me shake them off as Paul shook off the beast and felt no harm, Acts 28.

Anoint my head, Lord so the power will trickle down to my children and grand-children as the precious ointment upon the head of Aaron that ran down upon his beard to the skirts of his garment, Psalm 133:2.

Anoint my head, Lord so my helmet of salvation is always on. It is needed to protect my mind, eyes, ears, and mouth to remember, see, hear, and speak the laws, statutes, and commandments of You.

Anoint my head, Lord so I will always have a spiritual covering over it.

Anoint my head, Lord so every strand of hair will cause beauticians to desire a close or closer relationship with You, Jesus.

Anoint my head, Lord so beauticians will feel Your power upon me, causing yokes of bondage to be broken.

Anoint my head, Lord so beauticians are given revelation of Your word and answers to their problems while styling my hair.

Anoint my head, Lord so beauticians are given unique hair styles just for me as their hands are in my head.

Anoint my head, Lord so as beauticians are washing my hair, they will hear the voice of You Lord, upon the waters, receiving a Rhema word, Psalms 29.

Anoint my head, Lord so blessings may be upon it to sell valuables You have given me; not keeping them to myself to be cursed by the people, Proverbs 11.

Anoint my head, Lord with oil, so my cup will continuously run over.

Lord, all of these things I ask in the name Jesus, Amen.

ANOINT MY MIND, LORD

Jesus, as I place oil upon myself:

Anoint my mind, Lord so I will not entertain thoughts of doubt and fear the enemy brings.

Anoint my mind, Lord because it directs the operation of the whole armor of You, Ephesians 6.

Anoint my mind, Lord so I may quickly think to bow to worship You.

Anoint my mind, Lord so I will think on Heavenly things first and not upon things of the Earth.

Anoint my mind, Lord so I am not easily upset, but when I am, I'm able to handle matters rationally, quickly, spiritually, and with wisdom. Your word tells me I am mightier than a city when I rule my spirit; controlling my temper, Proverbs 16:32.

Anoint my mind, Lord so I may recall sermons in times of need; so I may remember bible class notes, Sunday school lessons and scriptures I have studied to direct or comfort me or to encourage others.

Anoint my mind, Lord so I may think to call Your name Jesus in my storms before I call upon my spouse, best friend, spiritual leader, or parent.

Anoint my mind, Lord so I may think to pray about my problem first prior to posting a message on the internet, displaying it to the world.

Anoint my mind, Lord so strongholds are pulled down, imaginations are cast down, and any high thing that exalts itself against the knowledge of You, 2 Corinthians 10.

Anoint my mind, Lord so I may think to praise and worship You daily.

Anoint my mind, Lord so when trouble taps on my window, I am not troubled, but strengthened by Your word.

Anoint my mind, Lord so I may think to read Your word daily even if it is placing my bible on the passenger seat of my car, reading verses at traffic lights.

Anoint my mind, Lord so I may think to do that which is right when my flesh desires to do that which is wrong.

Anoint my mind, Lord so I will not think unrighteousness is pure.

Anoint my mind, Lord so I will not think adultery is attractive and fornication is acceptable by You.

Anoint my mind, Lord so I will not think light stealing, white lying, a little lust, every now and then envy, juvenile jealousy, secret pride, minute rebellion, a hint of hatred, and a spoonful of porn is righteousness and acceptable by You.

Anoint my mind, Lord so I will think to walk in the spirit of humility daily and not in pride.

Anoint my mind, Lord so I will remember to boast and brag on You when my child earns excellent grades and not brag on my child. Help me remember it is You who created the mind to understand and retain information. It is You who gives strength in the hands to write and type. It is You who protects from danger in route to class, during the day, and in route home. It is You who provides food and drink to strengthen bodies. Lord, help me remember to thank You for all You do through my child. Also, help me remember to thank You for the great work the instructors do for and with my child.

Anoint my mind, Lord so I will think to pray immediately when the spirit of pride sneaks upon me.

Anoint my mind, Lord so I will not think a little gossip or a little slander is harmless.

Anoint my mind, Lord so when I think it is okay to be angry for extensive periods of time and having trouble apologizing, Your power will alter my thoughts.

Anoint my mind, Lord so I may think to consecrate myself by shutting down my friends and recreation, to be alone with Thee in prayer and meditation.

Anoint my mind, Lord so I may think to fill it and replenish it with Your word.

Anoint my mind, Lord so I may think to call a fast when I need answers to difficult situations.

Anoint my mind, Lord so I may think to call a fast when I need loved ones saved.

Anoint my mind, Lord so I may think to call a fast for healing and deliverance for myself and others.

Anoint my mind, Lord so I may remember to call a fast and to call on the name of Thee before calling on the name of my pastor, friend, or my educated child.

Anoint my mind, Lord so when I think I am greater than others, I am reminded that we are nothing without You. We are not used by You in pride, only in humility.

Anoint my mind, Lord so I may think to look up for my Redeemer lives, and not give up regardless to the situation.

Anoint my mind, Lord so I may remember to put all my trust in Thee and not in man. Lord, You said to put no confidence in man.

Anoint my mind, Lord so that I may think to thank You for all things.

Anoint my mind, Lord so that I may remember to give You honor, praise, and glory for all that You do, all that You have done, and for all that You are about to do in me.

Lord, all of these things I ask in the name Jesus, Amen.

ANOINT MY EYES, LORD

Jesus, as I place oil upon myself:

Anoint my eyes, Lord so I may identify You in the worst behavior of others.

Anoint my eyes, Lord so I may see the goodness of You in the darkest situations.

Anoint my eyes, Lord so I may see me as You see me.

Anoint my eyes, Lord so I may see what the end shall be for my life.

Anoint my eyes, Lord so I will view sin as sin.

Anoint my eyes, Lord so when the glory fills the room, it is seen, along with the miracles, causing me to hearken even the more to Your greatness.

Anoint my eyes, Lord so I may continue to see Your light and continue to walk in it.

Anoint my eyes, Lord so I may see the beautification of Your wondrous works done through myself, so I am continuously enlightened with revelation from You.

Anoint my eyes, Lord so when I close them, You will show me dreams and visions with revelation.

Anoint my eyes, Lord so I may focus on seeing Your face in Heaven as I seek Your face on Earth.

Anoint my eyes, Lord so I may see in the Spirit things that are, things that were, and things to come.

Anoint my eyes, Lord so I may see my situation changing before it changes.

Anoint my eyes, Lord so I may see myself healed before I am healed.

Anoint my eyes, Lord so I may see myself set free before I am set free.

Anoint my eyes, Lord so when I see trouble coming in the spirit, I may cancel it in the spirit.

Anoint my eyes, Lord so I may see myself financially solvent beforehand.

Anoint my eyes, Lord so I may see Angels in my presence and recognize them.

Anoint my eyes, Lord so I may witness miracles, signs, and wonders (fresh oil pouring from the ceiling and
through the cracks of walls, gold and porcelain teeth created in my mouth, gold dust resting upon me, glory clouds hovering in my home and car).

Anoint my eyes, Lord so I may witness the lame run and not just walk.

Anoint my eyes, Lord so I may witness dry bones come to life.

Anoint my eyes, Lord so I may witness the healing of people in hospice.

Anoint my eyes, Lord so I may witness the healing of hospital patients who have been given up by doctors.

Anoint my eyes, Lord so I may witness the blind receiving sight.

Anoint my eyes, Lord so I may see my spiritually lost loved ones found.

Anoint my eyes, Lord so I may see myself more compassionate like You.

Anoint my eyes, Lord so I may witness the aged women teaching the younger women to behave in holiness, to love their husbands and children; to be keepers of their home; to be discreet, and not false accusers, Titus 2.

Anoint my eyes, Lord so I may witness the aged women acting their age and dressing their age.

Anoint my eyes, Lord so I may witness the unmarried women caring for the things of You Lord, that she may be holy both in body and in spirit.

Anoint my eyes, Lord so I may witness the married women caring for the things of her husband, how she may please him.

Anoint my eyes, Lord so I may witness men caring for his wife, how he may please her.

Anoint my eyes, Lord so I may witness the unmarried men care for the things that belong to the Lord, how he may please the Lord.

Anoint my eyes, Lord so I may see pastors feeding their sheep more with things of You and with fewer things of the world.

Anoint my eyes, Lord so I may see the youth desiring holiness so they may live with <u>You</u> eternally.

Anoint my eyes, Lord so when You reveal truth, I will accept it and act accordingly.

Anoint my eyes, Lord so that I may diligently seek righteousness to procure favor.

Anoint my eyes, Lord so I may witness the youth respecting their elders and the elderly so they may be blessed by You and given longer life spans.

Anoint my eyes, Lord so I may see parents parenting their children more.

Anoint my eyes, Lord so I may witness more unity within churches, homes, and work places for strength.

Lord, all of these things I ask in the name Jesus, Amen.

ANOINT MY EARS, LORD

Jesus, as I place oil upon myself:

Anoint my ears, Lord so I may hear Your voice more distinctively than the voice of the enemy.

Anoint my ears, Lord so I may hear You as You are leading me in the path of righteousness.

Anoint my ears, Lord so I may hear Your voice upon water from the shower, pool, fountain, lake, sink, river, or beach to receive guidance, wisdom, and revelation from You, Psalms 29.

Anoint my ears, Lord so gossip will not enter me as a negative, but as a positive by causing me to intercede in prayer for individuals named in the gossip and for the deliverer of the gossip.

Anoint my ears, Lord so that I will hear You say, "Seek My face".

Anoint my ears, Lord so when I hear Your instructions, I will take heed to them without hesitation.

Anoint my ears, Lord so I can hear Your distinguished voice instructing me when I am sitting under the utterance of false preachers, teachers, and prophets.

Anoint my ears, Lord so I can hear the sighs of the hurting, the impoverished, the depressed, the incarcerated, and the back sliders so I may easily and quickly pray for them.

Anoint my ears, Lord so I can hear the yokes of bondage breaking; the shackles of sin liquidating; and the hardened hearts softening.

Anoint my ears, Lord so I may hear Your voice as You speak Rhema words to me; words of wisdom, and words of knowledge and act on them.

Anoint my ears, Lord so I may literally hear chains broken and shackles loosened of those in bondage as I pray.

Anoint my ears, Lord so I may hear You calling my name as I am in the midst of others with the same name.

Anoint my ears, Lord so I may hear You praying for me as You did Peter.

Anoint my ears, Lord so I may hear of Your glorious works and Your manifold witness on world news, then listen to the testimonies of unbelievers.

Anoint my ears, Lord so I may hear Your word with understanding.

Anoint my ears, Lord so I may hear counsel and receive instruction.

Anoint my ears, Lord so I may hear music pleasing to You; so I may listen to music that makes me think on Heavenly things.

Anoint my ears, Lord so I may hear the sound of an abundance of rain.

Anoint my ears, Lord so I may hear demons say, "Jesus I know and Paul I know, and I know you too.

Anoint my ears, Lord so I may hear instructions from my pastor, physicians, and parents and receive them.

Anoint my ears, Lord so I may incline them to hear the words of the wise to expand my knowledge.

Anoint my ears, Lord so I may hear myself praying to You, praying for others, praying the Word, and praying in the Spirit.

Anoint my ears, Lord so I may hear Angels speaking for me.

Anoint my ears, Lord so I may hear false teachers, preachers, and prophets repenting for deceiving many.

Anoint my ears, Lord so I may hear myself speaking the truth in my heart before speaking the truth from my mouth.

Anoint my ears, Lord so when I hear of wars and rumors of wars, I am not troubled.

Anoint my ears, Lord so when You stand at the door and knock, I will hear it, then open it so You may come in to sup with me and I with Thee.

Anoint my ears, Lord so when I hear You say, "Hear ye and give ear," I will stop what I am doing to listen and adhere.

Anoint my ears, Lord so when I hear You say this battle is Yours and not mine, I will surrender.

Anoint my ears, Lord so when I hear You say to cast all my cares upon You because You careth for me, I will no longer carry that weight.

Anoint my ears, Lord so when I hear You say love my husband, though I am abused, I will love him. You said vengeance is Yours, You will repay.

Anoint my ears, Lord so I may hear the secrets of Thee.

Anoint my ears, Lord so when I hear You say to abused husbands, "Love your wives", I will hear testimonies of them doing so, and sharing how You rectified their marriages, Your way.

Anoint my ears, Lord so when I am verbally abused, I am not affected mentally and emotionally, but healed by Thee speedily.

Anoint my ears, Lord so that I may incline them unto wisdom and apply my heart to understanding.

Anoint my ears, Lord so I may hear my enemies treading upon my turf afar off causing me to immediately fight in the spirit.

Anoint my ears, Lord so I may stand still and consider the wondrous works of Thee.

Lord, all of these things I ask in the nam Jesus, Amen.

ANOINT MY MOUTH, LIPS, AND TONGUE, LORD

Jesus, as I place oil upon myself:

Anoint my mouth, lips, and tongue, Lord so I may boldly call evil spirits by name out of individuals, setting them free.

Anoint my mouth, lips, and tongue, Lord so I may boldly declare Your word when faced with conflicts, rather than speaking a language unlike You.

Anoint my mouth, lips, and tongue, Lord so I may declare blessings over myself and others and not curses.

Anoint my mouth, lips, and tongue, Lord so I may speak creative miracles such as porcelain, gold, and silver teeth mouths where there are none.

Anoint my mouth, lips, and tongue, Lord so I may speak creative miracles such as new hearts, lungs, and kidneys.

Anoint my mouth, lips, and tongue, Lord so I may speak creative miracles such as fingers, hands, and arms.

Anoint my mouth, lips, and tongue, Lord so I may speak creative miracles such as toes, feet, and legs.

Anoint my mouth, lips, and tongue, Lord so I may speak creative miracles such as the restoration of hair.

Anoint my mouth, lips, and tongue, Lord so I may speak creative miracles such as money in wallets and bank accounts.

Anoint my mouth, lips, and tongue, Lord so I may speak creative miracles upon myself and others.

Anoint my mouth, lips, and tongue, Lord so I may not be rash with my mouth, being careful about what I utter before Thee.

Anoint my mouth, lips, and tongue, Lord so I will speak excellent and right things.

Anoint my mouth, lips, and tongue, Lord so I may speak Your word with boldness and clarity.

Anoint my mouth, lips, and tongue, Lord so as I speak, Your power rests upon each word that proceeds out of my mouth, healing many.

Anoint my mouth, lips, and tongue, Lord so that I am satisfied with good by the words spoken.

Anoint my mouth, lips, and tongue, Lord so when I cry unto You with my voice, then shall my enemy turn back, this I know, You are for me.

Anoint my mouth, lips, and tongue, Lord so whatever I speak it will be acceptable unto Thee.

Anoint my mouth, lips, and tongue, Lord so as I speak, Your power rests upon each word that proceeds out of my mouth, comforting many.

Anoint my mouth, lips, and tongue, Lord so I may pray Your word, pray in tongues, pray in secret, pray when my flesh wants to slander, and pray when I am unctioned to lie.

Anoint my mouth, lips, and tongue, Lord to empower me as I pray to pull down strongholds on the phone or internet, in writing, or in person.

Anoint my mouth, lips, and tongue, Lord so I may speak things I know and testify to the things I have seen.

Anoint my mouth, lips, and tongue, Lord so I will not call bitter things sweet and sweetness bitter; good things evil and evil things good; light things dark and darkness light.

Anoint my mouth, lips, and tongue, Lord so when I speak Your word, it will be like as a fire, and like a hammer that breaketh the rocks into pieces.

Anoint my mouth, lips, and tongue, Lord so when I speak, empty souls will be filled with Your spirit.

Anoint my mouth, lips, and tongue, Lord so I may bridle it during times I need to be quiet. Lord, You said, "Be ye not as the horse or as the mule, which hath no understanding: whose mouth must be held in with bit and bridle, lest they come near unto thee," Psalm 32:9.

Anoint my mouth, lips, and tongue, Lord so I will not eat the bread of wickedness nor drink the wine of violence.

Anoint my mouth, lips, and tongue, Lord so I may use it when it should be disquieted.

Anoint my mouth, lips, and tongue, Lord so I may speak Your word as a sword to teach, exhort, rebuke, and preach and not use it to belittle, degrade, hurt, or ridicule.

Anoint my mouth, lips, and tongue, Lord so I may speak, giving soft answers which turns away wrath.

Anoint my mouth, lips, and tongue, Lord so that I may speak at the appropriate times to keep my soul from troubles.

Anoint my mouth, lips, and tongue, Lord so that I may speak peace.

Anoint my mouth, lips, and tongue, Lord so that I speak not into the ears of the unwise because he will despise
the wisdom of my words.

Anoint my mouth, lips, and tongue, Lord so that I won't answer a matter before it is spoken to me; it causes shame and foolishness.

Anoint my mouth, lips, and tongue, Lord so when I speak, power permeates the room bringing deliverance, healing, and miracles.

Anoint my mouth, lips, and tongue, Lord so that when I pray, my voice shall come nigh unto Thee and whatsoever I ask in Your name, You will do.

Anoint my mouth, lips, and tongue, Lord so I may speak to mountains and they are removed.

Anoint my mouth, lips, and tongue, Lord so I may speak to storms and they are yet calm.

Anoint my mouth, lips, and tongue, Lord so I may speak to the winds and the sea and they obey.

Anoint my mouth, lips, and tongue, Lord so I may speak to sinners and they run to the altar.

Anoint my mouth, lips, and tongue, Lord so that I will quickly apologize with sincerity when I am in error.

Anoint my mouth, lips, and tongue, Lord so that I am not a tale bearer nor tell secrets spoken to me, nor a whisperer, destroying friendships.

Anoint my mouth, lips, and tongue, Lord so I may speak to the lame and they run, leaping over walls.

Anoint my mouth, lips, and tongue, Lord so I may drink waters of my own cistern and running waters out of my own well.

Anoint my mouth, lips, and tongue, Lord so that as I minister in song, power penetrates the listeners as of fire, burning sin, breaking yokes of bondage, and loosening shackles.

Anoint my mouth, lips, and tongue, Lord so I may speak to the dumb and they talk and sing to You.

Anoint my mouth, lips, and tongue, Lord so I may speak to the spiritually and naturally blind causing them to receive sight.

Anoint my mouth, lips, and tongue, Lord so my voice is heard by You early in the morning as I am directing my prayers to Thee.

Anoint my mouth, lips, and tongue, Lord so when I sing for You, souls are saved, healed, and delivered.

Anoint my mouth, lips, and tongue, Lord so when I speak to co-workers on my secular job, their thoughts, behavior, and conversations change.

Anoint my mouth, lips, and tongue, Lord so I will thank You in spite of. I will praise and worship You when it is cloudy or sunny, when I am prospering or insolvent; rejoicing or mourning.

Lord, all of these things I ask in the name Jesus, Amen.

ANOINT MY HANDS, LORD

Jesus, as I place oil upon myself:

Anoint my hands, Lord so that I am more like the tree planted by the rivers of water, prospering in everything I touch.

Anoint my hands, Lord so when I touch trouble, it dissipates.

Anoint my hands, Lord so when I lift them toward Heaven, I am totally surrendering to Thee.

Anoint my hands, Lord so when I high five my neighbor, as our hands touch, the glory will splatter in slow motion and wherever it rests, rather upon people, the pews, or the floor, cause an explosion.

Anoint my hands, Lord so You may teach them to war, breaking bows of steel with my arms, teaching my fingers to fight, Psalm 18.

Anoint my hands, Lord so that I will write on the table of my heart to never forsake mercy and truth.

Anoint my hands, Lord so I may be constructive with them (building) and not destructive (tearing down).

Anoint my hands, Lord so I will willingly pay my tithes to receiving blessings upon blessings from the windows of Heaven, Malachi 3.

Anoint my hands, Lord so I will willingly give my time, gifts, and offerings to the Kingdom.

Anoint my hands, Lord so the work of them is blessed and my substance is increased.

Anoint my hands, Lord so they may be strengthened to do great exploits for You.

Anoint my hands, Lord so I am rewarded according to the cleanness of them in Your eyesight, Psalms 24.

Anoint my hands, Lord so when I clap them, the sound of Heaven is heard as a trumpet, to call the unsaved and back sliders to the altar.

Anoint my hands, Lord so when I lay hands on the sick they will recover.

Anoint my hands, Lord, allowing heat to flow through them as I lay them upon others for healing.

Anoint my hands, Lord so when I hold the hands of others, power transfers to them causing healing in their bodies.

Anoint my hands, Lord so when I wave them, Your presence is felt by all in my company, bestowing blessings upon them.

Anoint my hands, Lord so when I carry Your word, I shall not drop it.

Anoint my hands, Lord so when I shake hands I will transfer knowledge, wisdom, and understanding into their hands.

Anoint my hands, Lord so whatsoever I do, it is done with all my might, heart, and strength.

Anoint my hands, Lord so I can easily give to others and serve others without hesitation.

Anoint my hands, Lord so I can open them to receive from others, accepting blessings as blessings and not as handouts.

Anoint my hands, Lord so I may lay them on check books and paychecks decreeing and declaring increases.

Anoint my hands, Lord so as I pass by hospital rooms of patients, they are healed when I lift them.

Anoint my hands, Lord so when I shake the hands of a wife, she takes on the spirit of the virtuous woman,
Proverbs 31. She will assure her family has food. She will work willingly with her hands. She will buy fields. She will plant vineyards. She will be filled with strength, honor, and wisdom. Her tongue will become the law of kindness. She will always be busy. She will stretch out her hands to the poor. She will reach forth her hands to the needy. Her kids will call her blessed. Her husband will praise her, and she will fear You. She will become the wife You would have her to be; loving her husband and full of submission.

Anoint my hands, Lord so as I type e-mail letters, texts, tweets, or posts, Your power causes recipients to feel You and act accordingly.

Anoint my hands, Lord so as I prepare meals, I will stir, slice, mix, bake, grill, boil, or fry more of You into my recipes, leaving the consumers desiring more, though they will think the desire is for more food, but it will be for more of Thee.

Anoint my hands, Lord so when I embrace someone I will squeeze encouragement and healing into them.

Anoint my hands, Lord so as I carry the weight of others, it will not wear me down or tear me down, but I am able to release it to You easily.

Anoint my hands, Lord so I am strengthened to hold my shield of faith without ever putting it down.

Anoint my hands, Lord so I can sternly hold my sword, which is Your word, to swing quickly in times of trouble, enlightening, teaching, and comforting.

Anoint my hands, Lord so when I shake the hands of a husband, he will have a greater desire to love his wife as Jesus loves the church.

He will become the husband You desire him to be; giving, forgiving, providing, comforting, and protecting his family.

Lord, all of these things I ask in the name Jesus, Amen.

ANOINT MY FEET, LORD

Jesus, as I place oil upon myself:

Anoint my feet, Lord so wherever I stand, I am standing more firmly on Your promises.

Anoint my feet, Lord so wherever I stand, I am standing in truth.

Anoint my feet, Lord so as I walk, my shadow is seen, healing people as they glance at it.

Anoint my feet, Lord so that I may walk in the spirit of humility and not in pride.

Anoint my feet, Lord so every step I take draws me closer to Thee.

Anoint my feet, Lord so I may stand on the grounds of many nations, proclaiming Your name, Your power, and Your word with boldness.

Anoint my feet, Lord so I may follow peace with all men.

Anoint my feet, Lord so that my footsteps are enlarged as I place them on the ground as I walk causing me not to slip.

Anoint my feet, Lord so I can run through troops and leap over walls, never to look back like Lot's wife, but press forward.

Anoint my feet, Lord so that I walk not in the counsel of the ungodly nor stand in the way of sinners.

Anoint my feet, Lord so I may continuously walk uprightly before You, walking in the path of righteousness.

Anoint my feet, Lord so I may tread on the enemies turf with boldness, declaring the power in Your name.

Anoint my feet, Lord so as I stand, I am standing in righteousness and standing in readiness.

Anoint my feet, Lord so as I walk through the valley of the shadow of death, I will fear no evil, Psalm 23.

Anoint my feet, Lord so when You place them "up" upon a rock, higher than my enemy they will not be able to reach me.

Anoint my feet, Lord so my steps are ordered in Your word, Psalm 37.

Anoint my feet, Lord so my shoes are continuously shod with the preparation of the Gospel of peace, Ephesians 6.

Anoint my feet, Lord so that I may walk with wise men which brings me wisdom.

Anoint my feet, Lord so when I step into a bus, train, car, or plane, the atmosphere changes and hearts change immediately.

Anoint my feet, Lord so as I walk into the room of chaos, the atmosphere changes to peace.

Anoint my feet, Lord so when I walk into a room of strife, all things come to order.

Anoint my feet, Lord so when I step into waters of trouble, they become purified.

Anoint my feet, Lord so when I walk in the midst of trouble, not only will You revive me, but You will stretch forth thine hand against the wrath of mine enemies, and thy right hand shall save me,
Psalm 138.

Anoint my feet, Lord so when they are planted in righteousness, my footprints are left for others to receive understanding, knowledge, and healing.

Anoint my feet, Lord so in my absence, people will know I was there because they came discouraged, but Your presence upon me lingers and they become encouraged.

Anoint my feet, Lord so when I walk, You are beside me, before me, and over me, guiding my feet with Your light, rod, and staff.

Anoint my feet, Lord so I may run and not be weary, walk and not faint.

Anoint my feet, Lord so they are like deer feet, pivoting through my trials and leaping over my persecution.

Anoint my feet, Lord so they are kept from falling so I may walk before Thee in the light of the living, Psalm 56.

Lord, all of these things I ask in the name Jesus, Amen.

ANOINT ME, LORD

Jesus, as I place oil upon myself:

Anoint me, Lord so my lungs are infused with so much power, whereas I inhale more of You and exhale anything unlike You.

Anoint me, Lord, allowing your power to flow through me as I pray, so when Satan thinks to speak to me, he will back up.

Anoint me, Lord so as others stand in my shadow, they are healed as it was with Peter.

Anoint me, Lord allowing your Glory to rest upon me so heavily that others walk past me and are delivered. When folk stand near me, they will feel your Glory and are healed.

Anoint me, Lord so I am able to wear my whole armor at all times to stand against the wiles of the devil.

Anoint me, Lord so I will not operate in fear or doubt as I await manifestations of Thee.

Anoint me, Lord so that I will continuously abide in You and Your words abide in me so when I pray, You will
answer me.

Anoint me, Lord so that whatsoever I do, I will do it heartily as unto You, and not unto men.

Anoint me, Lord so I will never fear what man or flesh can do unto me.

Anoint me, Lord so when I thrust my arms, Your power will go forth, healing and delivering everyone in the area.

Anoint me, Lord so when I smile someone will receive revelation from You.

Anoint me, Lord so when guests sit in my home, they are relaxed, encouraged, and enlightened.

Anoint me, Lord so my heart stays pure; only the pure in heart shall see You.

Anoint me, Lord so I will delight myself in Thee at all times.

Anoint me, Lord so ideas, suggestions, nuggets, knowledge, wisdom, and thoughts overwhelm me to enhance ministries.

Anoint me, Lord so I may choose You over anyone or anything always.

Anoint me, Lord so I may fear to walk unholy. You commanded us to be holy because You are holy.

Anoint me, Lord so my spirit is fed continuously with Your word.

Anoint me, Lord so when my darkest hour arrives, I will remember that darkness is Your secret place and run to meet You in my secret closet.

Anoint me, Lord so when my enemies fall, I will not rejoice and when they stumble, my heart will not be glad. Your word says to rejoice when others rejoice and mourn when others mourn.

Anoint me, Lord so I will always desire to reverence You.

Anoint me, Lord so my breastplate of righteousness is securely fastened, guarding my vital organs; my heart, lungs, liver, and reproduction system. My heart must be pure to reside in Heaven. My lungs must inhale You and exhale foolishness. My liver must keep my blood cleansed and I must be able to reproduce the things of Thee. You said the works that You do shall I do also and greater works than You shall I do if I believe on You.

Anoint me, Lord so my cry will come unto Thee causing You to come out of Your holy hill to save me.

Anoint me, Lord so my ways are pleasant and my paths are of peace.

Anoint me, Lord so I may be a tree of life to them I closely interact with.

Anoint me, Lord so when I lay down I will not be afraid and my sleep shall be sweet.

Anoint me, Lord so Your glory rests upon me as I speak, causing many listeners' lives to be changed.

Anoint me, Lord so the glory will fill the place where I am, causing many to receive blessings simultaneously.

Anoint me, Lord so that I will not withhold good from them to whom it is due, when it is in the power of my hand to do it.

Anoint me, Lord so the glory will appear in my office, causing co-workers to fall upon their faces.

Anoint me, Lord so that a light from heaven will shine around me as it was with Saul, Acts 9.

Anoint me, Lord so that the light You commanded to shine out of darkness will shine in my heart giving me the light of the knowledge of Your glory in the face of Jesus.

Anoint me, Lord so in times of trouble, I will be hidden in Your pavilion, in the secret of Your tabernacle.

Anoint me, Lord so my soul is delivered from death and my feet are delivered from falling so I may walk before You in the light of the living.

Anoint me, Lord to seek people to pray for.

Anoint me, Lord to seek situations to pray about.

Lord, all of these things I ask in the name Jesus, Amen.

AFTER WE PRAY

After we pray, which is talking to the Lord, we need to listen to Him. We desire revelation, direction, instructions, and answers to our needs from Jesus directly, but we must find time or make time to listen to Him. Though we receive answers from the Lord through our pastor, spiritual counselors, ministers, books, the Bible, friends, children, songs or television, there is nothing like receiving a word directly from Jesus Himself. It is something special about the Lord singling us out just to speak into our spirit. This is how I learned to hear from the Lord. As a child I heard from Him often and followed His direction. I just did not know who was speaking. I was quiet, always alone, and had no distractions. Therefore, I could hear the Lord loudly and clearly. When I grew up, I heard Him, but nothing like I used to. When I became distracted by the cares of the world, friends, clubs, dating, smoking, drinking, fitting in, fashion, cars, and the like, that separated me from hearing the voice of the Lord on a regular basis. Please do not misunderstand me. The Lord still spoke to me to warn and inform me, but I could not hear Him as often. It took years for me to hear Him as I used to. The Lord gave me revelation knowledge on how to hear Him again and on a daily basis. I am sharing it with you today!

Psalm 29:3 - The voice of the Lord is upon the waters: the God of glory thundereth: the Lord is upon many waters. The voice of the Lord is powerful. When I read this, the Lord taught me the power of His voice; what His voice could do. I learned that His voice causes trees to stretch out on the ground and cause flames of fire to divide. If you strike a match or flick your lighter, the Lord's voice alone can divide the flames. His voice can shake the earth. His voice directs wild animals to their meals. His voice causes hail and snow to melt. His voice causes the earth to be watered for vegetation, water for the animals to drink, and fresh tender grass for the sheep to eat. His voice is powerful and it is upon the waters. Therefore, knowing this, sit by the waters with your notebook and listen for a word from the Lord. Get a fountain and allocate time every day to hear His voice. I do not have a fountain yet, my fountain is the kitchen sink. I turn on the faucet and let the water run while I pray, while I read the Bible, or while I am listening to the Bible on compact disc. I sit in my living room and commune with my own heart while the water is running. I turn on the water in the bathroom when I enter. Out of habit, I turn the water on in the bathroom while I am looking for something in the cabinet or applying make-up. Haven't you heard of people saying that revelation or songs come to them while showering? That is the water; that is the voice of the Lord upon the waters. Haven't you heard people say the fountains at the spa are serene? That is the voice of the Lord. Isn't the Lord of peace? When you plan to meet the Lord daily, at the same time, at the same place, He will meet you there. He wants you to recognize His voice. He does not want you indecisive as to who is speaking to you. If you practice this technique, His voice will become distinct just as your spouse's voice, your child's voice, or your friend's voice. You are able to recognize their voices only because you have spent time with them. Sometimes I change my voice when my kids call me. They say, "Mama, please, I know your voice." This is how we ought to be when Jesus speaks. When He directs us, no matter the person's voice He uses, we ought to say, "Lord, I know your voice." I encourage you to turn your water on. Are you in a position to turn it on now? Put the book down and finish reading it with the water on. The Lord is not going to speak while we are speaking; that is not communication. He wants us to hear Him. This is how He does me. He speaks in between the words I pray or in between the words I speak or sing. He speaks during those still moments. When I am quiet, He speaks. When people say, "Can I ask you something?" I respond and say, "Yes." Then I immediately say to Jesus, but to myself, "Speak through me Lord." As the question is being asked, the Lord is speaking to me, bestowing upon me a wise response even if it is for me to get back with them later. I said the Lord speaks to me when I am quiet, not when the speaker is quiet. Remember, the Lord is not going to over talk us and He is not going to fight to get a word in.

If we exchange our University master's degree in *Talking* for a Business School certificate in *Listening*, we would be dangerous.

Turn over your plate! Pray up! Pray often! Listen up! Keep looking up! Turn the fountain on!

Thank the Lord for Anointing you today!

Be Blessed,

Brenda B. Matthews

www.ingramcontent.com/pod-product-compliance
Lightning Source LLC
Chambersburg PA
CBHW031437040426
42444CB00006B/855